Perfect As You Are

Understanding & Accepting Children with Disabilities

Written & Published By: Amanda Soria

ISBN-10: 0-578-40697-7
ISBN-13: 978-0-578-40697-8
LCCN: 1-7133273921

Printed in the USA

Dedicated to my boys, Ayden & Ryan.
I hope you never lose your sense of adventure and your love for others.

Special thanks to God for entrusting me with this special story, to my dear husband for believing in me, to Lisa for your encouragement, to Ezzy for inspiration, to Diane for your knowledge and to Shavel for your creativity.

Ayden and Ryan set out on an adventure.
Little did they know what they were going to find –
all sorts of new friends of different kinds.

So off to school they went...

First, they ran into Ezzy.

Hi, why are you walking with a cane?
Do you need help walking down the lane?

I was born blind so I cannot see.
But we are still the same, you and me.

I might not see the world like you do.
I can still smell flowers and hear music too.

A simple hello is all it would take.

In the end, all I want is a friend to make.

As they continued ahead, Ayden and Ryan said...

It's so great that we met; and we hope you never forget:

God created you from the top of your head to the tips of your toes.
He loves you more than you will ever know.
You were made with a purpose and in His eyes you are flawless.
Just as He made each and every star,
He made you, PERFECT AS YOU ARE!

The next friend they met was Kash.

Hi, we have a little dog too!
Why do you look and speak differently than we do?

I was born with Down Syndrome so I look and
talk a little different, you see.
But we are still the same, you and me.

Other kids never know what to say.
Sometimes they even get nervous and look away.

I just want to feel accepted and not set apart.

Please listen to the words that I speak from my heart.

As they continued ahead, Ayden and Ryan said...

It's so great that we met; and we hope you never forget:

God created you from the top of your head to the tips of your toes.
He loves you more than you will ever know.
You were made with a purpose and in His eyes you are flawless.
Just as He made each and every star,
He made you, PERFECT AS YOU ARE!

Right around the corner was another
new friend named Nora.

Hello, why do you need a walking aid?
We're here to help, don't be afraid.

I was born with Spina Bifida and it's hard for me to run, you see.
But we are still the same, you and me.

Just because it's hard for me to walk, doesn't
mean we can't talk.

I can play and even share.

All I want to know is that you care.

As they continued ahead, Ayden and Ryan said...

It's so great that we met; and we hope you never forget:

God created you from the top of your head to the tips of your toes.
He loves you more than you will ever know.
You were made with a purpose and in His eyes you are flawless.
Just as He made each and every star,
He made you, PERFECT AS YOU ARE!

At the stop sign, they met another new friend, Gracie.

Hi, can we join you for your walk?
Why do you use your hands when you talk?

I was born deaf and cannot hear, you see.
But we are still the same, you and me.

Sometimes kids point and squeal but
they don't know how I feel.

You can smile or even wave.

A little attention is all I crave.

As they continued ahead, Ayden and Ryan said...

It's so great that we met; and we hope you never forget:

God created you from the top of your head to the tips of your toes.
He loves you more than you will ever know.
You were made with a purpose and in His eyes you are flawless.
Just as He made each and every star,
He made you, PERFECT AS YOU ARE!

They saw another new friend that they could
make named Nathan.

Hey, we love to play basketball too!
Why do you need a wheelchair to help you?

I was born with Muscular Dystrophy and need help, you see.
But we are still the same, you and me.

As I sit here in my chair, all people do is stare.

I still love games and like to play.
Making a new friend always makes my day..

As they continued ahead, Ayden and Ryan said...

It's so great that we met; and we hope you never forget:

God created you from the top of your head to the tips of your toes.
He loves you more than you will ever know.
You were made with a purpose and in His eyes you are flawless.
Just as He made each and every star,
He made you, PERFECT AS YOU ARE!

They were almost to school when, they met
another new friend, Aiden.

Why are you so annoyed?
Is there something you're trying to avoid?

I was born with Autism so it's harder to stay focused you see.
But we are still the same, you and me.

Don't make fun of me or call me names.
I'm just a kid who loves to play games.

If you have questions, let me know.

Just please don't let hurtful words overflow.

As they continued ahead, Ayden and Ryan said...

It's so great that we met; and we hope you never forget:

God created you from the top of your head to the tips of your toes.
He loves you more than you will ever know.
You were made with a purpose and in His eyes you are flawless.
Just as He made each and every star,
He made you, PERFECT AS YOU ARE!

While out on the playground, Ryan got picked last for kickball.
All the kids said it was because he is so small.

As he was just about to get mad, his new friend
Kash said don't be sad...

Did you forget?

God created you from the top of your head to the tips of your toes.
He loves you more than you will ever know.
You were made with a purpose and in His eyes you are flawless.
Just as He made each and every star,
He made you, PERFECT AS YOU ARE!

Meet the Characters

Meet Ezzy! Ezzy was born partially blind and completely lost all sight by the age of 9. Her favorite color is red since that was the last color she was able to see. She loves her family, going to church, cooking and reading Braille. Her favorite hobby is creating beautiful jewelry.

Meet Kashton! Kash was born with Down Syndrome. He is an adorable 8 year old that is a big brother to two younger brothers and one sister. He loves swimming, playing his guitar, riding his bike and all things Spider-Man!

Meet Nora! Nora was born with Spina Bifida. She is a spunky little 3 year old who loves to play. She loves having tea parties with her baby doll; her favorite color is pink. When Nora grows up she wants to become a teacher.

Meet Gracie! Gracie was born in China and was adopted at 19 months. Born Microtia Artesia makes her hearing impaired. She wears a device called Cochlear Baha that allows her to hear. Gracie loves making clothes out of paper and cardboard. She loves to craft, sing, dance and swim. She also loves to ride her scooter and jump on trampolines.

Meet Nathaniel! Nathaniel, an 11 year old boy, was born with Duchene Muscular Dystrophy and Autism. He loves to swim, travel and go to Disneyland. He loves to play with his two younger sisters. When Nathaniel grows up, he wants to be a surgeon.

Meet Aiden! Aiden was born with Autism. He is an 8 year old boy who loves to joke around and have fun. He loves Spider-Man, roller coasters and going fun places. He loves to play with other kids and really wants to have friends.

Meet Ayden and Ryan. They are brothers and are the best of friends. They love going to church, playing football and reading books. Their favorite thing to do is to meet new friends and go on daily adventures. When they grow up, Ayden wants to be a Pastor/Principal and Ryan wants to be an architect.

Meet the Author

Amanda Soria is a God-fearing woman, a devoted wife and a loving mother of two boys. Amanda's mission in creating this book is to carry out the message to God's children that you are "Perfect As You Are" and to see all of God's creations through His eyes.

Glossary

Blindness - Blindness is strictly defined as the state of being totally sightless in both eyes. A completely blind individual is unable to see at all. The word blindness, however, is commonly used as a relative term to signify visual impairment, or low vision, meaning that even with eyeglasses, contact lenses, medicine or surgery, a person does not see well. Vision impairment can range from mild to severe. Worldwide, between 300 million and 400 million people are visually impaired due to various causes. Approximately 50 million people are totally blind, unable to see light.

Down Syndrome - A common birth defect that is usually due to an extra chromosome 21. Down syndrome causes intellectual disability, a characteristic facial appearance, and multiple malformations. It is associated with a major risk for heart problems and a minor but significant risk of acute leukemia. Treatment for Down syndrome includes early intervention to develop the mental and physical capacities to their utmost, speech therapy, and surgery, as needed, to repair malformations. About one-half of children with Down syndrome have heart defects, most often holes between the two sides of the heart.

Spina Bifida - A birth defect and a type of neural tube defect that involves an opening in the vertebral column caused by the failure of the neural tube to close properly during early development. Since the defect is in the spine, part of the spinal cord is exposed and protrudes out. People with spina bifida often have neurological deficits below the level of the lesion and can suffer from bladder and bowel incontinence, limited mobility (due to paralysis of the legs), and learning problems. In the US, spina bifida occurs in 1 in every 1,000 births. The risk of spina bifida can be significantly decreased if women take ample folic acid before and during pregnancy.

Microtia Artesia - Microtia is a congenital deformity in which the external ear is not completely developed, occurring in one of every 5,000-7,000 births. Microtia is almost always accompanied by atresia, also known as aural atresia, a condition in which the external auditory ear canal is either absent or closed. Medical professionals aren't sure exactly what causes this deformity, but believe it occurs during early pregnancy when the soft tissue of the outer ear and middle ear are being formed.

Duchenne Muscular Dystrophy - The best-known form of muscular dystrophy, due to mutation in a gene on the X chromosome that prevents the production of dystrophin, a normal protein in muscle. DMD affects boys and, very rarely, girls. DMD typically appears around the age of two with weakness in the pelvis and upper limbs, resulting in clumsiness, frequent falling, an unusual gait and general weakness. As DMD progresses, a wheelchair may be needed. There is no cure for DMD. Current treatment is directed toward symptoms, such as assisting with mobility, preventing scoliosis, and providing pulmonary therapy.

Autism - A spectrum of neuropsychiatric disorders characterized by deficits in social interaction and communication, and unusual and repetitive behavior. Some, but not all, people with autism are non-verbal. Autism is normally diagnosed before age six and may be diagnosed in infancy in some cases. The degree of autism varies from mild to severe in different children. Children with autism have trouble communicating. They have trouble understanding what other people think and feel. This makes it very hard for them to express themselves either with words, through gestures, facial expressions, and touch.

* Adapted from www.medicinenet.com

12730562R00020

Made in the USA
San Bernardino, CA
16 December 2018